DOOR TO MY SOUL

ANUSTHA PAL

ISBN 979-888591119-1

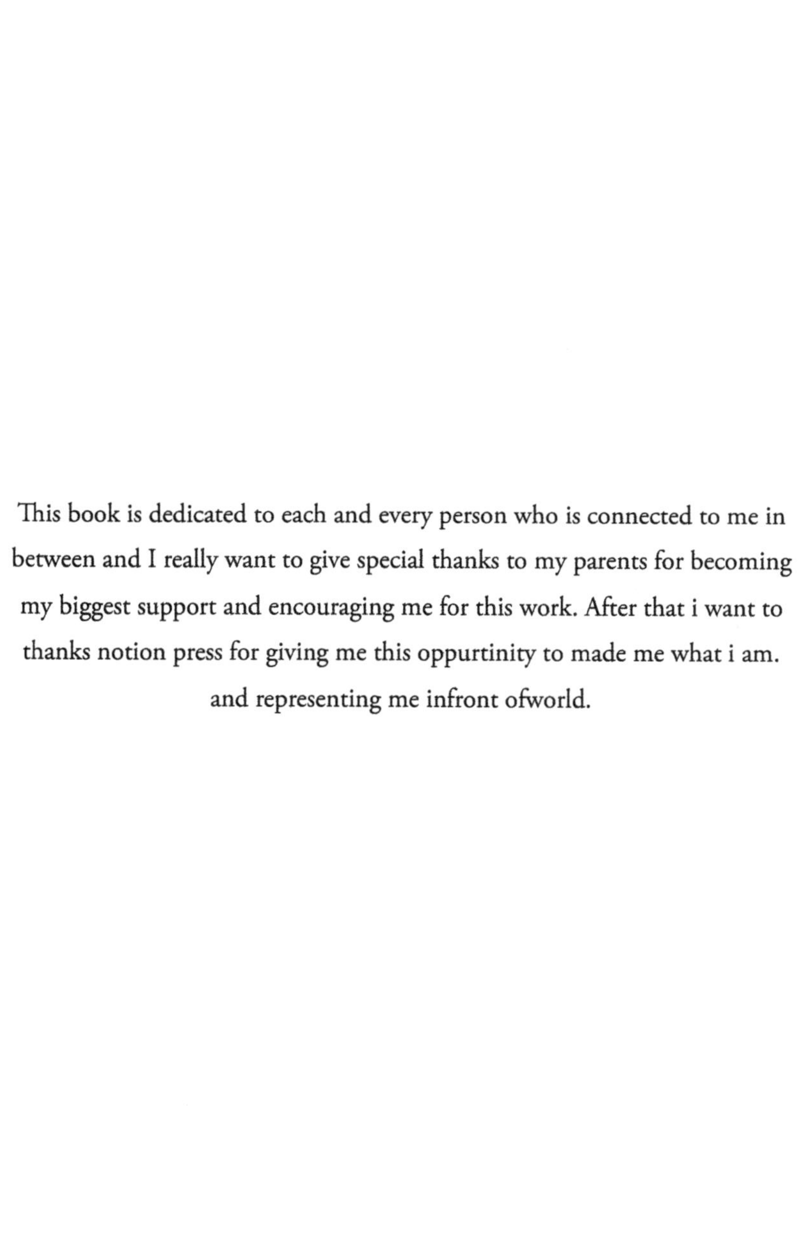

This book is dedicated to each and every person who is connected to me in between and I really want to give special thanks to my parents for becoming my biggest support and encouraging me for this work. After that i want to thanks notion press for giving me this oppurtinity to made me what i am. and representing me infront ofworld.

Contents

Contents

Foreword

Author of this book Ms. Anustha Pal, started her work when she was 19. she took her graduation in Bachelor of technology in computer Science, that is too Far from writing but she knew and define her writings and poetry in that time that make her publish her thoughts and vision in the form of poetry book. Her parents and people around her inspire her to write what she feels And her uncle Virendra Pal also inspire from her books started publishing and writing. She inspires people around her from being a beautiful Poet. she wrote amazing books - Scars that is too intresting to Read.

Preface

This book is the collection of wonderfull feelings which are not easy to tell or to express. But we all belong to this. According to me feelings is something very hard to resist. Like if you are sick so you having so if anybody ask so you directly tell that you are sick, but behind that many feelings hidden which are difficult to express. Which only our soul can feel. I come out with this book to take you to a soulfull journey.

Feeling of love contains thousand unexplainable feelings which are like different shades of a single colour love. So took you deep inside the world of feelings, through my poetries you can feel relax mentally. basically I love to write in between the lines which took a hard to understand but that are the key to take your soul too deep and intense. I hope you all enjoy reading this book.

1. SYMPATHY

When there's a situation
Smearing over you like the
Drops of rain
You have some fizzy hair
But they are not shining
The level of thinking n
Some patchy thoughts
All lead to sympathy.
Sympathy of whom?
Is of your lover, or of your father.
The desires and glimpses of
the past and fearfulness are
stubborn reasons to lead to sympathy.
Is caring is sympathy??
Or sympathy is caring
People give felicitation
For your pleasure
And sympathy for ur care.
Suzy asked her brother
Not to regret, and all that
Lefts are sympathy.
People asking my wet window
To stop falling your pearls
And give some delicate sympathy.

Darkness when all around me,
And I see fringes dazzle
I have got sympathy.
Life follows sympathy
It's coming to each,
It's come to teach the
Existence of honesty.

2. LOVELY TRUTH

To be in your arms
To be in your mind,
No guilty feelings,
That you left in me.
You are just a star Too far, I feel crushed by your
Astonishing eyes.
You wear charms in you
I wanna drown me down in your deep thoughts;
The integrity of your thought
Steal my beautiful heart.
I believe in your inner Beauty,
Your colors touch me
At that angle on which,
I was never able to bend me Down.
Your luminosity is crashing My heart.
Your love is never-ending
Because I don't keep just it
In my mind but in soul and My heart.
Your love will not vanish
It's my philosophy that never
Make me feel that
now i am without yourlove.

3. SENSATIONS

Something which
Assembled in one class
Sometimes, shattered in
different parts.
it's just like a brook
Flirt and play with the breeze.
It has tiny twinkle eyes
To smirk in love.
Something lefts undiscovered.
It changes the tang which never
stop mesmerizing.
It's something imperishable
Sweet like eyes, soulful and
Essencefull But still
Something left undiscovered
You go through.
Droop down your honesty
It's not probably as simple as others think,
It's something habitat in your spirit.
You can find out something
Remarkable,
you Astonishing and creating atmosphere,
to take my brown eyes
You can't steal the helmet of

Anxiety, because it is not in
my eyes.
Wear something which,
make you walk under the stream and
Over the sky to touch my hidden anxiety and clear my mind.
Don't just stop,
Justify your time of quality.
Don't let you smile,
otherwise, your smile will kill me.
May probably next second
Your heart stop beating
If you really don't feel.
Smile is something natural. Not a burden,
It's my real gift.

Wear a dress of grace to
Enhance your time to get back to real life.
please dont think too much i always live in your eyes.

4. SLAP

The power of your arm, reach their clever ends,
you drop on my face.
the magnificence of
my Face found no
reason to stay.
the valley of my insane red roses oppose your praise,
And palm of hand fought
Against the hit, you make on my face.
When we lose all suspicion and hope from your wings.
I fly away.
No reason to stay.
When the notion of arm give
Me a shape.
You deliver your attitude
on my simplicity and grace.
I don't wish but remember
You are dominant everyday.
When everything my esteem
fall Down but your arm tells me
that I am wrong.
But you treat me without any courtesy
And now I am living with no emotion
but a fake smile on my face.
At that moment I expense all my Life.

It's your hand and me.
To give me an intent to get Scared .cause,
Insecurities hire me like
Vehicle daI and do damage to my respect.
Now you know my complexion It's not so bright.
Podium of my voice falling
It's dignity so it doesn't come out.
All Prosperity and infinite things i adjust.
It's not just a slap it's tell that i am a bluder.

5. CHESS

Missing the plunges of rain
Staying for the gown within
That I came in,
Grass Valley with butterflies whimper
In the visions.
Pursue my ache, my buddy
And Companion
Without my small steps,
I am never the winner of Real chess.
My rooks are fighting by
Running in lines to kill the opposition.
They took the position of
Proposition.
Knights are supervising
From every night.
Their fighting spirit make
Opposition relatives away
From my point of time.
Bishop forms the triangle of
Fighting strategy.
Diagonal dimensions assassin
Tell about the real strategy to
Use on peers.
Pawn is the safeguards

Patrols every opponent.
Whenever a woman like
I get hurt by statements
Of Dogs,
They heal me every time.
By king is very different
Don't need any effort that's
Why he took only one step.
I am the queen and a real
Player for which everyone
Endeavors.
I talk buttery with my own flaws
That's why my queen is dead
But on the board, I have to stay
My gleaming novice is on duty,
They are my proud they are fighting
For this big opportunity.
I try hard to get my queen back
Step up my soldier but he waits a moment and stays,
He stays an instant, as per
He knows he has to save the Queen
For the help making the triangle
Knight reached.
Gave rise to an idea never born,
Take a move to kill the opponent.
I thought about the diversion
Putting my soul into him to get the solution.
In place of opponent I slew
My own beliefs.

Stop following my crazy past
Start my new present with gifts.
Getting back into my life.
I take a step forward make a queen and win the game.

6. YOU

When you see me
You want to collect my
Rolling tears,
And make me feel this drama you love.
And become smoke rising from A lamp,
To give directions.
When my identity is naked
The only thing that matters, is your soul.
nothing else like that for which I should wait.
my heart is crying
Out for help,
For all differentiation
I see Plunging into my lap.
My intention will
Change by long runoff Memories,
I become too Harsh and gravel-hearted.
Did you come?
For Die and deceased of me,
Believe me,
I never turn my eyes to forget these dreams.
you don't want to see my Misery and life
but still waiting for your words is my choice.
From the clock hands,
Black windows rough my every pore.

Now the last thing
I want to see is You?

7. APOLOGY

When every hail
Make semantics fall
Like drops of mist and
Fog.
But when I become the
cloud of apologies.
Sometimes holding the chunks
Is become the solution of every strategy.
But broken pieces can lead the
Oceans
there is no handsome pot which
Holds my flower pretty heart.
Fake blind c sentences
Only create cavities.
Which you can never remove the whole life you cross.
Apology holding the patience and realization
Give flowers to life .
The most important lesson
Comes in apologitic light.

8. RAINY FEELINGS

I found a moment fall,
It's yours and it's always yours.
A dream of being your
From internal winds creating power of emotions.
I just occasionally want your
Body tone, inside my curtain life.
That jolly polite and creamy.
I always admire your
Elegance and your light
I use it on the occasion of light.
I want your everything
to be mine.
I tumble for you, wait for
you every Minute
And don't go Because
for you my horologe.
Stop the chore,
Clocks are slowly vanishing
Love in your beauty admitting
That butterflies are
Flying above,
It doesn't matter that you are a secret
Or outside of my light.
I just love you through my Heart.

My beloved, you live inside
My gravity of light.
your dance in your rain my feelings
comes out in my tears.

9. FIVE FEET APART

It's you and me, Five feet Apart
a small distance with a million
wishes left underscore and draft.
A strategy of love is not clever
distances between us become an
obstacle but my heart will never change.
Giving rise to a cloud of wishes
And scars
move like a swing, but never
Tell about the feeling you get.
we are in love but still standing
Five feet apart.
Your distance I am unable to calculate,
Maths will never reach this stage,
It's hard to believe that you
I never see you.
You are just an imagination.
that's why you are standing five feet
apart in every pose.
your cloud virtuality,
Frozen the real world,
it's hard to imagine that
you actually exist.
i dream one night we are together,

But still we are standing Five feet aparts.

10. MY WORLD

How did it take me to
The edge of life,
How does gravity fail to Float
my mind in the sky?
Who'sthat Given boundaries to
My life rises to the kingdom of your gaze.
From My physique to soul
feeling uneasy but allure.
I am a free and liberal bird
But still, life is the thing I never
Explore.
If I started to find different
ways to get a new life.
But this cage never let
I enjoy the waves.
A moment which broke my illusion
In spite of being superstitious,
When my Vitality is taken In a broken doll,
it make me strrugle for gettting a life atlast
Broken doll gives a smile and
After this long I make me
Satisfied and now she become my world for life long.

11. SWEATER

I am knitting my sweater, All day long
Not even think that
knitting is not my passion at all.
Making the portrait of things You never know,
Searching peace in papers And Wisdom every time.
knitting all day long bringing rust to my bones.
but habits don't change without any storm.
You not relinquishing your
Focus on keeping reckless
Balls in your mind.
You by playing with your
Emotion and body it's cool
And but not right.
Knitting my wollen all day long,
Reaching the conclusion it's the
End of time.
Now my body temperature rises and
I am on the bed with a freaky fake smile.
and life is at threat, but
I am not having my husband to cure.
now responsibility and traps are revealing their truth.
I spend my whole life on them and waste
my reality and nature.
Before the sweater gets complete.

I lost my strings Now there is no other way.
Then I realize that
I was awry mountains peaks are in my
mind curved path make me faint the Moment let me know
I am living in the luxury
I never have.
tears coming again and
Again,
Moments doesn't admire
and i reach heaven.

12. FAILURE

I am not the history
Across which you
Can go through,
I am not an ingenuity
You can draw on your
Cardboard life. but brings tears
and broke you.
I am not a tale
Whichever comes true
I am a pale color.
Relinquishing the interest
In the names.
There are no colors of
Fantasy, which I can explore you are lucky
that I come to you.
All you have is a chasm.
Smiling in every failure,
Creates nonsense sound but still,
it forms images that make life amazing.
Failure is the events I write for Me,
Without them, I can be ever
Reach into the veins,
accepting, and practice
Is the Solution here.

Conclusion letting you
To came back.
repeat and practice make sense.
your nature doesn't change
the direction of success.
but working can bring reflection
which everyone respects.

13. REALITY

Watching storms taking
my Everything,
With his strokes.
spright looks reflect the honesty of Kings.
I am at my eighteen
Talking with my friends
Reality is what people hide.
in a Small mirror truth
Gives it's every reaction.
Never thought that it was just A reflection.
No way to measure interior reality Of someone,
but eyes sometimes tell everything,
It's a real statement.
I deserve a non painted history
A black n white dream,
A fake God,
No love only interfaces live Inside me.
but I never lose my reality.
Bring all my confidence
with an unexpected dream.
I come out with a style
Which faint everybody.
It's only my face flowering,
Everything falls on the ground In jealousy,

This is me.

My reality gets a beautiful end.

14. ILLUSION

To be in a false argument,
I awoke from my levels.
I don't know, what I know
How I getup early today
It is neither possible but
It is not an illusion anyway.
I washed my face and
give a smile to complete my day.
my reality washes every rebellious person.
my simple change their realism.

15. FALSE AWAKENING

dress me up the entirety,
I pose in front of the mirror,
Something awful I see
And I awoke!!!!!
I just decompress me
and Come out of bed,
set aside,
My nose starts to ooze.
It is hard to reckon, that
I don't cry.
I try to wrap that situation
But still l fall.
I ran to the medic but next
moment I am in the woods,
That's evolving in my head,
Ample it with uncertainty.
I feel juggling moments,
The events are out of control,
I heard a murmuring sound,
I am nervous but still go for it,
There exists a brook,
With the mystery of colors,
that I never understood,
I rubbed my eyes and try to analyze

But an unknown mystery that I own,
I see my degree across
the brook with a similar frock,
It's like I am standing in front of the
Reflection pool,
It's out of probability
It's a reckoned expression
My heart falls down,
Pointer sends to my limbs,
I run in the rush right side,
As fast As I can,
At a moment a realize that
It's nothing but a pseudo mind,
In simple letters false
awakening every time.

16. STRENGTH

Spread the smell,
Catch the frequency,
Small chapters make
Me a book.
I try to convey a speech
But I forgot that,
Whatever I am realizing
Is very difficult to Say.
But downfall gives me
Knowledge to bring chuckles
Around this is my actual strength
I am working for.
Maniac drama is at its
Superiority,
Survival for the fittest is not the phrase.
it's a strength of symbol.
use the tools given by
God and become powerful.
I am smearing And crashing
On these eyes everyday.
But making me
Dissatisfaction gives birth to vulnerability.
Walking on the road of
Life without obstacles is

an imagination wrong.
we live in the world of
probability strength is the only
event that probability one.

17. RIVER

Whenever I just sit
Besides a panorama,
The flow of the river is the first thing
that comes to our mind.
it just distracts my mind
I lose my focus,
remember the day we come close to us.
The dews are like pearls which
Are on my leaves.
Helfy Heavy rocks wrap
that extent.
Nature which belongs from
Motherliness of earth,
Culture and realms that all
Pertain to my dreams.
When the essence of the atmosphere
Reverse back,
with thunder and snow comes
Down with hail,
Dispersion moments are like
An image.
Some of the things that happen
We need a special eye to reach.
Beauty of the stream with white glacier is there,

but still, the canopy comes down to my knees.
I got some marvel feelings.I can't believe
it is the magic of the river which makes
her through our mind narrow and deep.

18. EMBARRASSMENT

Drama driving out of the
Scene,
Colour of aroma are changing
Like chameleon,
To get out of embarrassment
And hazards,
Situations letting me down.
Underground my viewpoint,
Let me fall in love with
This eternity,
The junction of highway is
Never be like that crowded
Like my brain,
It's all about embarrassment.
Talking pranks to some
Friends,
Indeed reckon balls are in
My mind,
Taking most tasty edibles
In my mouth,
Which makes my mindset reaches
Heaven apart.
But embarrassment is something
that never leaves's my head.

there is some embarrassment
which i never forget.

19. PROMPT

Start watching from the gazes,
In diamond demeanour domes
Of mind.
Tongue is out of peace,
We still fall for what,
We never Created for.
Prompt make mehis jester.
When the market down it's Rate,
Gave us the bargain but still Make us regret.
We will buy all the town out
In our head,
And when we realize, he prompt us.
When we scroll the Internet
Shop out venues of dress and
Other addresses,
They read out our aura,
But they never admit.
All we felt is, we are jester
Of their framework.
Now when we pray for someone,
But never get something Best,
But Without prompt
God gifts us Our parents.

20. BLUE HUT

The sky with colours ask
My magical stars,
Ask me what make you
Live for everyday.
Telling the world that
after several problems.
Painting the blue hut is
My everything.
Instead of being public face
Living under the stars makes
My face like a flower,
Fighting with reckon balls
And situation rolls me down,
Inspite of these situations
decorating my blue
Hut is my everything.
You are treasure of someone else
Temperature and honour
I can't Change.
Instead of having black business card
Living in my blue hut is my
Everything apart.
Love missed my something
In your table drawer,

Dreams ask me question about
Mybroken Pieces.
Living between the bad guys
Makes Butterflies high fly ,
But still leaving my everything
For my blue hut and
Decorating this hut is my Everything.

21. JESTER

We are invisible clown,
Laughing all the day and All the night.
Even when we don't
felt sufficient,
Then also we smile in our Silhouette,
When our emotions don't
Get enough and we shop
Out some behavior,
We smile in our phone profile,
Makes people feel joyous all The time,
Instead of being sad
From inside that laughing
Make you a clown,
We don't have a colored Nose,
We never wear a hat,
We don't do that kind of makeup,
But our exterior look is enough.
I always left in delima that
Is fake smiling is truly good?
I don't like it sometime,
But then I felt about parents
Why they also took,
On the beautiful smile of
Their children they

Flow like a brook,
Unnatural smile that a lover
Put up on their face to make,
Their partner the most happiest
Person on this earth.
Still passing bogus smile
Gives many thing to us,
It sometime brings real
smiles To others.
We are just a clown,
making people
Smile is our real worth.

22. CORNER

Saying sparks are on the head
Rain is gleaming and pouring
In sake of becoming fearless.
I shop my streets
But Only four corners trying
To Get my attention ,
This is my room, sometimes
Become place on inspiration.
They bring me out of every
Delima and pain,
Just by counting angles that
Four corners bring.
They now and see my everyday Reality,
They start loving me when
There is no one for me.
When I bring out my assertions
And nobody listen to me.
They are not just corners they
Are jury of my love which is insane.
They are dream, well-wishers
I never know and never read Before.
They are such dignity
Corners , took my every dream with them.
That tell me my wholestory in a

Single word corner

23. SNOW- A GOD FAIRY

The white appetite and theatre
Of snow,
Which making me to begin my
New journey,
I am the beginner and modifier
Of attitudes .
Snow, I never seen From
my entire life
But still I just think that I found
You some day in heart.
When you just come and
Pour on my heart,
Some symbol of dreams
And irony of continuous
Come out and cover all
My belief.
Your shape is epicenes of Beauty.
I learn some true hard lesson
From you.
But you just passed a long
Ridges of time to greet my Soul
You welcome me that's why
You are near to heart.
When you comes to me like

A dancing butterfly,
You fall and melts down all
The province of my complexion.

24. CLOCK

My clock started talking
To my time.
They convince my time
To stop one day.
Time ask where you
Want to reach?
I try to tell it my truth
But I want to heal my
Scars and burns
So I move it future.
Want to know about my Destiny.
I am having lovely children
And handsome Husband.
Beautiful and glorious life it's like
what I dream.
But time let me know,
they are Leaving me,
I faint in sickness and turn
My clock come back please
I want to make correction
For my guilty.
Then I see me in the
present Moment
Curiosity kill the cat and

I fall For My past just to make me
Feel what I am,
But seeing my reality I fill
My heart with some wounds
And anxiety
Then I ask my clock
What is my best time?
It was 12 noon when I am asking
My clock stop for that moment
Telling me the gifts of present.
Bring me something stunning which
Past and future can't give .
tell this is your best time
Because it is real.

25. PRECIOUS THINGS

You are my memory
Or a prison of wishes,
You are Halley's comet,
Who shows his beauty,
Once in seventy-five years.
Are you healing,
Or a silence that fades away.
You must be a distraction,
Who found intuition,
Insufficient Stamina through
My waves.
I heal down every pore but,
Still, your things affect me from
Every way.
I am confident and living still
With images
you are that precious thing
I carry in my pocket,
sometimes took you out under streetlight,
so that you shine becuase
you are the most precious thing for me.

26. END

I am at the end of your
clumsy and struggling,
I am massive and huge
Amuse and always comes
In a cycle and never stay.
gazing glances and
time clock makes you know
The criteria, era, and marvels.
You may be nervous
but I Come in every stage.
To know the prodigies of your events,
there is some notion Always stay.
This is not a closure,
Which you can create.
You are the eye of,
left pasture and wonder
history you write,
Knowing that you are no more
Beginning not to help you stay.
Ending makes everything
Visible, insight and until your day.
It's better to understand,
The nature of the game.
Ending tells the irony of

Your day and giving a
new Beginning of every black night
into a glorious morning.

Thank you so much for reading this book...

Printed by Libri Plureos GmbH in Hamburg,
Germany